THE TEENAGE WORRIER'S
POCKET GUIDE TO SUCCESS

Also available in the *Teenage Worrier* series,
and published by Corgi Books:

Pocket Guides
THE TEENAGE WORRIER'S POCKET GUIDE
TO ROMANCE
THE TEENAGE WORRIER'S POCKET GUIDE
TO FAMILIES
THE TEENAGE WORRIER'S POCKET GUIDE
TO MIND AND BODY

I WAS A TEENAGE WORRIER
THE TEENAGE WORRIER'S GUIDE TO
LURVE
THE TEENAGE WORRIER'S GUIDE TO LIFE

Also available:

THE TEENAGE WORRIER'S FRIEND
THE TEENAGE WORRIER'S CHRISTMAS
SURVIVAL GUIDE

THE TEENAGE WORRIER'S POCKET GUIDE TO SUCCESS

Ros Asquith

as Letty Chubb

CORGI BOOKS

THE TEENAGE WORRIER'S POCKET GUIDE TO SUCCESS
A CORGI BOOK : 0 552 146447

First publication in Great Britain

PRINTING HISTORY
Corgi edition published 1998

Copyright © Ros Asquith, 1998

The right of Ros Asquith to be identified as the author of this work
has been asserted in accordance with the Copyright, Designs and
Patents Act 1988

Set in Linotype Garamond by
Phoenix Typesetting, Ilkley, West Yorkshire

Corgi Books are published by Transworld Publishers Ltd,
61–63 Uxbridge Road, Ealing, London W5 5SA,
in Australia by Transworld Publishers (Australia) Pty Ltd,
15–25 Helles Avenue, Moorebank, NSW 2170,
and in New Zealand by Transworld Publishers (NZ) Ltd,
3 William Pickering Drive, Albany, Auckland.

The Random House Group Limited supports The Forest Stewardship
Council® (FSC®), the leading international forest-certification organisation
Our books carrying the FSC label are printed on FSC®-certified paper.
FSC is the only forest-certification scheme supported by the leading
environmental organisations, including Greenpeace. Our
paper procurement policy can be found at
www.randomhouse.co.uk/environment

MIX
Paper | Supporting
responsible forestry
FSC® C018179

Printed and bound in Great Britain by Clays Ltd, St Ives plc

Contents

L. Chubb, striding purposefully towards New Dawn,
Shining Beacon Etck.

Number Ten Downing St
The White House
Vatican
Buckingham Palace
Hollywood
Cannes
Yacht-on-Sea
Champagnesville
Lottery six zillion
I WON 100K
Universe
Eternity

Ye Bluebird
of SUCCE SS

Dearest Reader(s),

    As you see from my address above, my new-found confidence has led me to pen a guide somewhat different from my other glumey tomes. This is the El Chubb guide to having a fantastic SUCCESSful and totally excellent life-style, starting out with nothing but a couple of dried peas and a handful of grit. How is it to be done? I hear you cry. Peasy! Every single thing you need to know is right here in these dinky pages, pressed like dried flowers between the leaves of this unbeatable bargain buke. YES! Within its pages are clues to the following:

*   *How to get SUCCESS in everything you do.*
*   *How to enjoy SUCCESS when you've got it.*

* *How to be a millionaire, werld-famous*
  artist/leader/physicist/pianist Etck Etck.
* *How to be SUCCESSful in Lurve, Money,*
  Friendship, Exams, Business, The Arts, blah blah
  blah.

(If you believe all this, dear reader, you are not totally
SUCCESSful yet in telling ye difference between truth and
falsehood, but since most of our V. SUCCESSful people
share this failing with you, you are obviously well on road
to same.)

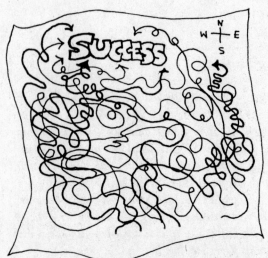

Just a few of the, er, many winding
roads to SUCCESS. Each of us has their
own path to find. For everyone a different
journey... blah, blah, blah.....

Akshully, as you wld expect if you have read my other bukes, you will know that I am not interested in savage, cut-throat, trample-everyone-else-under-feet approach to SUCCESS which Western World embraces. Instead, I yearn for a werld in which each yuman fulfills their hopes and dreams as best they can. And I sincerely hope that in writing it, I will find a way to both help you, fellow Teenage Worriers in the vineyards of glume, as well as moiself, to aim for stars while not minding plunging into pit full of snakes, sulphur and glue every now and then.

If I can do it, being most nervous person in history of World, then you can too.

Yrs, full of V. High Hopes (gulp, where's my Lucky Rabbit's foot?)

x *Letty Chubb* x

A FEW SHORT WERDS ABOUT SELF . . .

(for those of you who have not yet dipped into the world of L. Chubb.)

I am a fifteen-yr-old beanpole with hair like spaghetti and more spotz, cold sores and other festering protuberances than any other Teenage Worrier in the world. I have no sticky out bitz where they shld be, however. I am V. Lucky (I know, though usually forget) to live with two whole parents, although whether the term 'whole' can truly be applied to luny father who barely scrapes living but plays computer gamez all day and Only Mother who was born rich and spends all her time moaning about poverty-stricken state is a debatable question. Am currently dreading GCSEs and writing these bukes to make money so it doesn't matter that I won't get any. I have a V. Clever big brother (Ashley) who all my frendz fancy, but none of his frendz ever fancies me . . . and a V. Sweet-looking but bonkers little brother Benjy, who is scared of floors. My cat, Rover, is V. Old, but she is only person who truly cares about *moi*, I think. Apart from Granny Chubb, who still knits *moi* thingz all the time as though I were a baby, even though she can't see (which is obvious to anyone

4

looking at result of her knitting).

I am in love with Adam Stone, who fails to return my passion. You can read about him and the dastardly Daniel Hope in my other tomes (sob).

I am going to be a film director (notice how confidently I write that, it's part of my new plan: Not 'I want to be . . .' but 'I am going to be . . .').

And now, on with the true guide to SUCCESS . . .

(NB I still say 'banana' instead of that glumey word about dying that rhymes with 'breath'.)

ACHIEVING

SUCCESS in anything is about achieving and one of favourite teachers' terms is 'high achiever', 'low achiever' Etck. But to achieve, you need to know yr limits as well as yr capabilities. Anyone CAN learn ANYTHING if they try hard enough. But there's not much point, in view of El Chubb, in trying V. V. Hard at things you have zero interest in. You have to do this at first, to get right number of exams Etck, THEN find out wot you lurve, and go for that. Being good at something is 85% work and 15% talent, so not V. Talented people who are energetic, diligent Etck can do much better than V. Talented lazy people. (Must raise self from filthy bed and stretch eyelids).

ACTING

I did once dream of acting but my tragic experience as the Spirit of the Woodland in the Sluggs Comprehensive panto of *A Christmas Carol* served to convince me that performance is not my natural *métier*. (Incidentally, I often have a Dream that a V. Handsome Man with Hooded Eyes will come to the door one day and say he's come to read my métier, ha ha, however I fear my Adored Mother will get

GIGANTIC
with
Leonardo di Yum Yum
and
Letty Chubb
On second thoughts, maybe I shld tinker with my surname if going after star billing..

there first). However, in a play that made Tiny Tim a giant oak tree threatened by cruel woodcutter Scrooge, perhaps I could be forgiven for failing to shine. It may be that I have not yet found the right author to nurture my delicate talent . . . and life on the social security with an occasional end-of-pier performance might at least feel more SUCCESSful than just being on the social security permanently like most of today's yoooof . . . We can but dream.

ADVERTISING

will this subtle repetition werk?

The tricky thing about advertising is that the Advertisers know we think it's all Krap Etck but the idea is not to get us to believe the message but the message *behind* the message. This can be done by things happening on the screen or in the pic that you hardly even realize are there – or it might be a V. Clever ad that flatters you because it implies you must be Clever to appreciate it, or an ad with characters you get used to so it works like a Soap. However they do it, they're SUCCESSful at worming their way into yr soul. Worth checking out, learning tricks of trade and using for V. Good ends rather than just selling new can of beanz Etck.

BUY Another copy of this buke. Buy another copy of this buke. Buy another copy of this buke. Buy another copy of this buke. Buy another copy of this buke.

ANSWERS

Always beware a person, or group of people, who say they have The Answer. There is no one Answer and cultish lunies are likely to lure you into End-of-the-world-style missions that will obsess you, take all your time and may well end up driving you completely nuts. One of the only things I liked about times tables is that, once you learnt them, they always had the same answer. This is V. Comforting, but not true of much else in the werld. There are always many solutions to problems and the SUCCESSful thinker tries to come up with as many as possible and then chooses the best.

APPLICATION FORMS

Campaign for lessons at skule in how to fill these in and how to make the most of yrself, eg: if you have no GCSEs but six younger siblings – 'Very experienced with small children'. This means learning how to be positive without akshully lying.

Name: Letty Chubb
Sex: Not yet (sob)
Age: Fifteen

Arts

I find that art soothes the turbulent spirit Etck and
am probably happier when reading V. Good buke or
drawing picture than anything else. I also believe
that film is one of ye grate modern art forms and
that British film industry under Newish Labour
government might have chance to survive. To be
SUCCESSful in art, as in all else of any kind, you
have to work like maniac. It is not about drifting
dreamily and spouting verse, but about trying to
express yr feelings about the werld.

Beauty

Although Teenage Worriers think this a vital
element in SUCCESS in Lurve Etck, you only have
to sit on bus and examine occupants to realize how
V. Few of human race actually possess the kind of
beauty that we all seem to want. Yet, if you crack
joke, you will see each of yr fellow travellers' mugs
transforms from leaden inner-city (or deprived rural)
mask of glume into V. Nice expression of
merriment. This has more to do with beauty of
SOUL, naturally, and lots of people have this. If
Teenage Worriers cld forget about wanting to be
beautiful and concentrate more on beauty around us

– little birdies, flowers, grate Art, Etck – then they wld be happier. And being happy is V. Often the key to feeling SUCCESSful.

BEGGING

NB LIFE STATISTIC ALERT: three out of every five people you see sleeping on London Streets have degrees (makes you think you should get a job selling vegetables off the back of a barrow, eh?, instead of studying Etck. But this is a responsible buke and must look on Bright Side). Most SUCCESSful place to beg is apparently the City (where all the businessmen, guilty lawyers Etck hang out).

OR, you can sell *The Big Issue*. V. Hard work. Not for Teenage Worriers with roof over head. But it is much better to sell something than to beg, as it gives you some self-respect. Even in incredibly poor African countries, you usually see someone trying to sell one old piece of fruit off a box, rather than stoop to holding their hand out and expecting something for nothing.

BELIEVING IN YRSELF

It is essential (so I'm told, cringe, wail) to have high self-esteem in order to be SUCCESSful. Combing tomes about this subject comes up with all the corny old stuff about Standing Up Straight (impossible for banana-shaped person like self) Etck, but L. Chubb has condensed various volumes to give you V. Simple advice:

* Stand up straight (if poss).
* Express yourself.
* Sing really really really LOUD.
* Write lots of poetry about yourself, how you feel, how you look.
* Get your feelings OUT in the open.
* Think about all the great things about yourself and the people you love.
* Tell them. (Wow. Radical, huh?)
* Every time something bad happens, think of its good side if at all poss, or try V. Hard to remember something that is good, even if it happened ten years ago and nothing nice has happened since (wailing banshees, extra mournful violins . . .)

Birthdays

El Chubb's advice for SUCCESSful birthdays: between ages of 13 and 17, forget Birthday parties. Why put yrself through all the Worry of who will come Etck, and whether your parents will wreck it, or how loud the music can be, or whether a gang of gatecrashers the size of bulldozers will come in armed with knives and sell drugs to your baby sister? Instead, just nag your poor suffering folks to fork out a few quid for you to go to cinema or show with yr best frend, or out to fast food joint Etck. Then ask for V. Expensive presents and say how lucky they are not to have the kind of teenager who wants frends stamping fag ends into their carpet (my own parents do this anyway, but some of you probably live with houseproud adults). Then, when you're eighteen, you can get the BIG PARTY sorted out. And no-one can interfere . . .

BOOKS

El Chubb's advice: always have a buke on the go. When Worries crowd in threatening to suffocate the very life from yr glumey limbs, you can stave off the abyss by turning to read of the sufferings, joyz Etck of others. I feel that I shld be reading something a little more, um, sophisticated than the Famous Five, *moi*self, but I got V. Depressed by *Anna Karenina* so am giving self a little break. Thank heavens I did not give *Jill's Gymkhana* Etck to jumble sale.

Despite V. Good SUCCESS-type advice on de-cluttering, (poncey new phrase meaning 'tidying-up'), it is sometimes good for Soul to re-read cosy and comforting bukes that you enjoyed when you were but a happy child without the threatening Worries of impending adulthood, jobz

Etck. Books always tell you that someone has been here before, felt what you feel, Worried about your very own Worries.

I have to say also that, as you get older, you begin to value the ways these things are said too, viz: *I walked along on my own and saw a lot of yellow flowers* does not have quite the same ring as:

> '*I wander'd lonely as a cloud*
> *That floats on high o'er vales and hills,*
> *When all at once I saw a crowd,*
> *A host of golden daffodils . . .*'

(That's Wordsworth for all of those who go to skules about as good as Sluggs Comprehensive.) Appreciating langwidge is also V. Satisfying and can feed the Mind, *moi* thinks. It is also the key to SUCCESS in most fields of yuman life. And any of the many thingz I mention in this humble tome can be read about further in grate bukes – all available free of charge at yr local library.

BOREDOM

Is the enemy of SUCCESS. If anything bores you, ask yourself *why*. Is it cos you feel you are too old for it? Or is *it* too old for you? Or it's something you won't need to know about to pursue your chosen career as a belly-dancer? Fine as these reasons may appear to be, you will find that most SUCCESSful people are never bored. They probably started out by running messages, making tea and loads of other so-called 'boring' things and are always looking for hopeful Teenage Worriers that they can exploit rotten just like they were exploited themselves. Ask if you can do the boring stuff and pretty soon you'll find you get to do the fun stuff. If not, move on . . .

Next time you are bored, try to find *one* interesting thing that is happening (it cld even be thinking about why you are bored) and you will magically discover that the sedated sloth of time has turned into the winged hare . . .

L. Chubb sez: There is no such thing as BOREDOM. However, I make exception when encountering above.

BULLYING

It is V. Pathetic to want to hurt other people.
If you identify with any of the above, get help.

TIPS & HINTS

It can be V. Upsetting to be called names: fatty, skinny, slag, four eyes, smelly Etck are all wounding, especially if you feel they are true.

Try not to fall into the trap of always returning an insult, as you can just get into a slanging match that teaches the bully nothing and drives you crazy. People who are SUCCESSful and feel happy about themselves don't waste time slagging off other people anyway. It's the bullies who have the problems, and it's nothing to do with you and it's NOT YOUR FAULT. Here are a few replies you might like to try out in front of a mirror and then

16

even try next time someone gets rude. If you can't bring yourself to actually SAY them, then THINK them instead and it shld make you feel better:

'It takes one to know one.'

'The first sign of madness is thinking people with glasses have four eyes. The second sign is saying so.'

'You poor thing, you must be feeling really insecure to say that.'

'You'd never dare say that without your pals round you.'

'Hey! fancy you taking such an interest in the way I look – are you worried about the way YOU look?'

'I am naturally fat (or thin, or spotty, or whatever they said). You, know, like you're naturally rude.'

'Hey! Have you noticed that huge bogey dripping off your hooter?'

'Remind me to borrow you when I need someone to send me to sleep.'

'That's not what you said last night in bed.'

'Thank you for your inspiring remarks.'

'Funny, didn't know anyone with such a big head could have such a small brain.'

'Hang on, could you repeat that so I can write it down?' (This last one shld worry most bullies. They'll think you're going to report them.)

ALWAYS laugh or smile as though you haven't a care in the world. But DO tell an adult if anyone is really getting you down. DON'T suffer in silence.

17

CALENDAR

What a useful invention for Teenage Worriers!
With a calendar you always know where you are,
viz: to Whit, stuck on the dodgy old earth with a
whole day's Worry ahead of you before bedtime! My
Adored Father sometimes says they managed all
right in prehistoric times without calendars, but
since the days were all pretty much the same (get
up, bash spouse with club, bash passing mammoth
with club for lunch, lie down and have a nap, go to
cave with mates for Happy Hour before sunset, eat
more mammoth, bash spouse with club, go to sleep
Etck) a calendar wld have been a bit superfluous.
However, since organization is basic requirement of
SUCCESSful folk, getting a calendar and writing
your stuff in, is V. Good time-and-motion advice.

YIPEEEE! Got a
calendar! Booo
hooo! Got nothing
to put in it except
Cat's birthday

CAMPAIGNS

SUCCESSFUL CAMPAIGNING TIPS

1. Choose your subject. Ideally something you feel
V. Moved about, rather than just dutiful.
Alternatively, you can sneakily choose Ideals of one
who is close to your Heart, ahem. Who cares what
Adam likes? (And how am I to discover . . . ?)

2. Form campaign group. Rope in Hard-working
folk who are prepared to fold and lick things
(campaigners always need lots of leaflets, petitions,
Etck), but be sure not to phrase yr recruiting pitch
exactly like that or you will get a lot of those people
who are always responding to ads for French lessons,
big chests with fully opening drawers Etck. Try to
have at least one person who can spell, as V. Imp to
make your points in Literary style. Artistic persons
also welcome for logos, heart-rending pics of
starving yuppies (sorry, that shld read *Puppies*) Etck.

3. With your group, either join an already existing
organization or, if one doesn't exist (frinstance if you
are campaigning for something Local), form your
own.

4. Name your Group. Acronyms are V. Good here.
eg: El Chubb's very own CHAP (Campaign for Hairy
Arm-Pits), or a surprising name like ARNOLD for no
good reason other than that people will remember
it.

5. Have lots of meetings – V. Good way of asking V. Handsome (er, dedicated) Boyz to yr house.
6. Make posters, banners, petitions. Hope Gen Public does not observe irony of Yr 'Save Trees' slogans scrawled on millions of bits of paper.
7. Take same on marches.
8. Sell old rubbish to make funds (resist temptation to make this Joke about career path of Adored Father) Etck Etck.

As you see, campaigns present loads of opportunities to get out and about and feel useful to society at same time. Also, if you ARE V. Worried about the Environment, Animal Rights Etck, then you can FIND OUT MORE and also DO something about it.

CAREERS

One big Worry for Teenage Worriers today is that it's much harder to get good jobs than it was for our parents, eg: if you want to be a doctor, you already have to have fantastic A-Levels, have performed emergency heart by-pass surgery on yr Parents, starred in *Casualty*, written Hypochondriacs column in Sunday magazines Etck. And even when you have all the qualifications, you will often find that you also need to be grade 8 on the cello to prove you have 'other interests'. Gaaaaad.

This means you've just got to be V. Dedicated,

hard-werking Etck if you want to succeed in one of the secure professions. At this point, it is werth pausing for a moment to consider what the secure professions are: *Undertaker* is the only one *moi* can think of where one is V. Unlikely to run out of business, although it is hard to imagine a werld that won't need doctors, dentists and (sigh) lawyers, to enable the patients of the above to sue them for taking out wrong tooth, sawing off wrong leg Etck. Wait. *Accountancy* is another well paid, secure job, but *moi* thinks you need more exams for this than you do for undertaking or grave-digging, which only needs muscles. (NB Before training as grave-digger, though, check there isn't a V. Big move to cremation.)

Have just read above and must admit it sounds a bit glumey for a guide to SUCCESS, so will now put on fule's motley and cry from rooftops: try to find something you lurve and then try to think of a way it can actually earn you a living. The jobz situation, which has been V. Glumey for last fifteen yrs (whole of El Chubb's life, sob), is looking better in my crystal ball as I write this – and if you are doing something you lurve, you are much more likely to be a SUCCESS at it. SUCCESS, as you shld by now have realized, is not about fame and dosh, but about feeling good about yrself. And doing anything as well as you can, whether it's painting the yellow lines on the road or exploring Outer Space, can make you feel SUCCESSful.

CINDERELLA

This is a story about apparent SUCCESS which is, in ye humble opinion of El Chubb, a V. Bad example to Gurlz in Today's Society. She slaves away uncomplaining, nagged by V. Nasty Family, being dogsbody Etck. Then marries a prince just because she has small feet! I think such a cynical concoction of anti-feminism and shoe fetishism shld not be held up as a triumph of children's litritcher Etck. And as we all now know, marrying a Prince is not necessarily route to happiness either.

Stuff yer glass slipper. I'm off to be an Astronaut

Naturally, as I may well return to my ambition to be a nun and selflessly serve the community, I do not mean that Cinderella was wrong to devote her life to others, but she cld have chosen some middle course between serving her selfish old bats of sisters and disappearing off to a castle with a prince who is only interested in her below the ankles. *My* heroine is Granny Chubb, who worked V. Hard for a handful of old nail clippings and didn't grumble . . . (but I still think she shld have grumbled more – then she might have a decent pair of specs).

When I am Prime Minister, I will make sure Granny Chubb is rewarded and that Cinderella gets V. Good Edukashun to cast off shackles of Oppression Etck.

COMPUTERS

My Adored Father is V. Bad Example of what can happen if you let computers get on top for as readers will know he is a Hopeless Case of computer slavery to the dreaded computer game. His latest is UNIVERSE, where he plays the person who invented God(!) and creates thousands and thousands of different planets with different eco-systems Etck Etck. Though fun, this is definitely inhibiting him in the SUCCESS stakes, as he wld much rather do that than earn measly crust through writing for a living . . . But we must accept that though computers are throwing a lot of hardworking and decent folk out of work all over the place, they are only tools and it is up to the Moral Values Etck of the Human Race to decide whether they will be an influence for Good or Ill. If we cld only invent a programme to feed everyone in the werld for instance . . . Hmmmm.

CREATIVITY

Tapping into this magical force is essential for SUCCESS in most fields. Lots of Teenage Worriers assume that only artists are creative, but in fact creative thinking goes on in all businesses, and in all the sciences. Think how incredibly creative people who are looking for cures for diseases have to be!

Lots of Teenage Worriers think they aren't creative just because they've been told they can't draw or something stupid like that, when they were six, but most of us have a spark in us only waiting to be ignited. A good way to practise this essential discipline is to exercise those brain cells and do IQ-type puzzles, or to think of twenty ways to cross a river without a bridge . . .

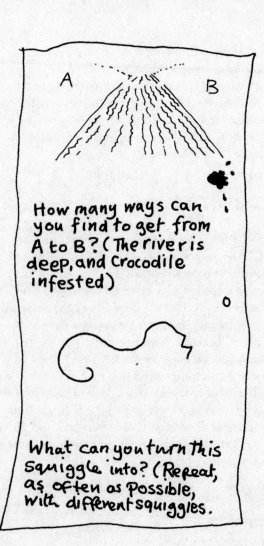

A   B

How many ways can
you find to get from
A to B? (The river is
deep, and crocodile
infested)

What can you turn this
squiggle into? (Repeat,
as often as possible,
with different squiggles.

This Elephant is standing in front of something. What?

Make up a song, draw a picture or write a story about the elephant, the river, a box of fudge and the squiggle.

INVENT a system of feeding and housing everyone in the world. Send it to The Prime Minister. (or to me - and I'll forward it)

DIAMONDS

Diamonds are often seen as symbols of SUCCESS. Akshully, though I am V. Unimpressed (ahem) with material trappings of wealth Etck, there is quite a good reason for diamonds to have value: they take a long time to form from carbon under deep pressure and huge temperatures in the seething bowels of the planet. SUCCESS, similarly, takes a long time to grow in seething bowels of Teenage Worriers, and is worth nourishing, searching for, and digging up in similar way to diamonds.

When you are a Middle-Aged Worrier, you may have diamonds by the score. (All you need is a diamond mine, thousands of exploited miners, a factory full of sawers and polishers and an absence of guilt!) For now, for *moi*, it's life that matters, not its superficial baubles. I would prefer just the burnished twig that Daniel gave me once with these tender words: *'Letty, when you no longer want to go out with me, you don't have to say anything. Just wear this through your nose and I will know.'* If only he had *meant* it . . .

DOCUMENTARIES

If you wish to have a SUCCESSful understanding of the werld, you should watch lie-on-the-wall (sorry, that shld be fly-on-the-wall) documentaries. These are the serious bits of TV that the BBC occasionally still puts out after they think everyone has gone to sleep. They tell you what is akshully going on in Werld Out There rather than about whether the latest soap opera star is a junkie or not or whether two Big Gurlz in American football kit can whack each other off a high wire with inflatable cucumbers, and if you are engaging in intelligent discourse (which of course, if you are reading this humble tome, you must be) you will need to gen up on info of this kind, so that when someone asks yr opinion on whether we shld sell arms to Indonesia, you will not enquire whether they've had an outbreak of leprosy in the district.

DYNAMISM   zoooooM YES?

One of the words most often associated with SUCCESS. Dynamic people are often thought to be those who work till midnight, party till 2 a.m. and are up fresh as daisy with lark to throw themselves anew into mind-spinning activity of buying and selling shares, arms factories and small countries Etck. If they are in the arts, they will be the directors of several opera houses and yet still have time to make deep and meaningful films about the true Meaning of Life while dictating their biographies and directing two thousand naked thespians in groundbreaking spectacle based on history of time and space.

Any Teenage Worriers who feel like curling up to die, giving up all hope Etck on reading this should pause to consider that only V. V. V. Few SUCCESSful people are actually this dynamic. There is an inner dynamism that even the average spot-laden, snoozing, slovenly Teenage Worriers can find, and it's to do with tuning in to the thing you like doing best. Frinstance, a boy who is never seen to rise from bed till three in afternoon can transform to whirlwind of activity when put in front of drum kit, Etck.

As a general rule, however, trying to do a *lot* rather than a *little*, is the best rule for cultivating dynamic-type personality. Say YES to new stuff, rather than putting it off till another day, and you cld find strange little strands of dynamism magickally sprouting from yr nut . . .

Emotional Intelligence

This is a new catchy werd for wot the mothers of the human race have been doing for centuries — that is, responding intuitively to other members of human race and negotiating pitfalls of loathing, cruelty, glume Etck by understanding human frailty and avoiding its worst excesses. Developing Emotional Intelligence is obviously hard for those apparently born without it (I name no names, but many werld leaders seem to be afflicted this way), and there are several bukes about that are worth dipping into to see if you've got it or not. Obviously it is possible to be rich and powerful without it (in fact, it may be obligatory not to have it) but if you want a SUCCESSful life as imagined by L. Chubb, which means a happy and fulfilled one, then this is for you.

I think we'll have to cultivate his EMOTIONAL intelligence

2+2

Environment

Have you any ORGANIC Fudge?

Looking after the planet is going to be the key to the SUCCESS of humanity's survival or not. Therefore, going into any form of ecologically friendly work is going to be good both morally and in terms of your own SUCCESS as a member of Yuman Race. Even big banks and world conglomerates are now being forced to take a bit more care of the werld and the voice of every humble Teenage Worrier can make a difference. So: CAMPAIGN for organic food, clean fuel, saving water, cancelling Third world debt (where poor countries are spending more on paying back rich countries than they are on feeding their own people!) and other V. Good things. SUCCESS, predicts L. Chubb, will surely follow.

Exams

Sadly, the passing of exams is seen to be essential for SUCCESS in today's cruel grinding werld. It is V. Important to try V. Hard to do this while at the same time realizing that many SUCCESSful people were NOT good at skule and flourished in the even crueller market-place of life by using different parts of their brains and body. In El Chubb's talent-frendly Yuniverse, you should not need exams for art skule or music college or drama skule or sport – all you should need is to be good at these things and full of enthusiasm. But unfortunately you DO need exams. So, to pass them:

EL CHUBB'S EXAM TIPS

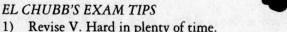

1)   Revise V. Hard in plenty of time.
b)   Ask your teacher what bits you need to work on most.
3)   Do the most and best coursework you POSSIBLY can.
D)   Get a V. Good 'How to pass exams' style guide – there are loads of these about.
e)   Read the questions carefully.
f)   Be sure to answer the right number of questions.
7)   Do the bits you are confident about first and then go back and fill in the others, but be sure to leave time.

8) Go to bed V. Early and eat V. Healthy food for two weeks before big exams start.

9) Do not despair if you do badly. You have yr whole life ahead of you and these horrible daze will seem like nothing then (so they say, arg Worry Etck). Seriously, there are many tragick cases of Teenage Worriers being pushed so hard by themselves or, more likely, by Middle-aged Worriers, that they completely freak out over exams. The key to SUCCESS here, is to do as above and then RELAX.

Phew. Summer!

FEELINGS

Adults always say that growing up SUCCESSfully is about getting your feelings and your judgement balanced so they don't keep going up and down like a seesaw. But some Middle-aged Worriers, espesh the ones you read about in the papers who order terrible things to be done in wars, or keep people in prison just for disagreeing with them, or even just fire people who've worked for them for years, or fax messages to their BeLUVREds saying sorry but they've met somebody nicer, don't seem to have any feelings at all, or if they do they keep them locked up in one part of their lives and don't let them spread around and get in the way.

Which is why in my less Worried moments I'm glad I have a lot of Feelings, even if they're often a Nuisance. I spend a lot of time and energy not just Worrying about *moi*self, but about how other people are feeling about something I've done or want to do, and maybe when I'm older I won't Worry about that so much and leave them the room to make their own minds up without me doing the Worrying for them. But without all these feelings sloshing about, you wouldn't be able to feel happy about yr SUCCESS, would you? Or the SUCCESS of people you lurve? All you would have is a kind of tarnished gloating, so wot wld be the point?

FRIENDS

There are Middle-aged Worriers and Teenage Worriers on the planet who call themselves sociopaths. These are people for whom frendz and frendship have no meaning and I am not one of them. These people are often V. SUCCESSful in a way, as they have never been hampered by the feelings of others but have just gone their own sweet (or sour) way. They have loads of time, too, as they are never on the phone for hours to someone who has just been left, sacked Etck. They are the ones who *do* the leaving and the sacking. If this is the kind of SUCCESS you want, then you are probly reading the wrong buke.

If you are fond of other people but worried that they do not return yr feelings, first check out that they are not sociopaths. If they are just ordinary Teenage Worriers, then smile hopefully, show an interest and you may find they like you too. There's no point in trying to be frendz with everyone – that wld just make you like a little dog that wags its tail pathetically whenever it's patted. But having a few really close frendz is V. Good for a SUCCESSful life in the opinion of El Chubb, even if it does take time away from being grate artist Etck.

Everyone has moments when they feel rejected or alone but it is V. Sad when the ones you wish to engage with you in the rich tapestry of life are indifferent to you. It does not mean they dislike you, simply that they do not really notice you – or are just too busy with their own lives. If, despite all your wiles, manoeuvres Etck, the Frend of Your Dreamz still says 'Hi, it's great to meet you' when you're in the midst of initiating yr sixth conversation with them that week, give it just one last try. Wear Outfit opposite (whether you are a Boy or a Gurl). No response from your Dream Frend means Indifference. Retire gracefully and seek Partners new.

Part of a decent SUCCESS plan is learning to take the slings and arrows of indifference on the chin. (I don't know why they say 'the chin' – the slings and arrows seem to hit me in all parts of the Bod at once). If this was all our chins had to put up with,

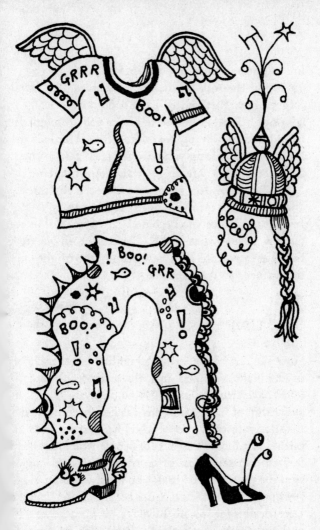

If you seriously consider actually wearing this,
you may qualify for
a) Lottery grant for the Sartorially Challenged.
b) Medical Attention.

life might be a bowl of peardrops.

Run-of-the-mill indifferences includes: Best frend forgetting yr Birthday (if parents do this, seek adoption); Teacher failing to notice you although yr hand has been waving pitifully in the air for half an hour; Mother asking you how you spell your name Etck. This is just life, so get real, stop whingeing Etck. (Boo hoo.) Almost always someone you care about will turn up. And loyalty to old pals is V. Imp. If by chance you become V. SUCCESSful or famous, never forget yr pals. They will turn out to be more important than new people who might only like you cos you're rich.

Guns

Since the terrible shootings of children at the school in Dunblane, Scotland, in 1996, attitudes toward Guns have changed in the UK and private ownership of most handguns has now been banned, despite protests by people who like blasting away at birdies, cardboard cut-outs of people who look like Saddam Hussein Etck for sport. But this does not stop the prob of what to do about the celebration of the gun in Movies Etck. Guns seem to fulfil V. Deep desires for Instant Revenge, settling probs without paperwork, meetings Etck, making the weak feel powerful and the powerful even more powerful. Worse still, it is poss at times to sympathize with these feelings. But I dread to think what might have happened if the only kind of SUCCESS you could have would be at the end of a gun. Banning all guns is a hopeful dream of L. Chubb. But who knows, if our generation Teenage Worriers can get SUCCESSful enough to rule werld, maybe we can get rid of them for good? We can only try . . .

Happiness

Happiness is something the Yuman Race strives for. Although impossible to identify except when you are experiencing it, it is thought by many to be the key to a truly SUCCESSful life. People look for it in different ways, and believe different things are stopping them from getting it. Benjy strives for Happiness by not stepping on the floor if he can help it. Horace (Benjy's hamster) strives for Happiness by going round in his wheel (his potential for Happiness is of course somewhat more restricted than his Ancestors, by being shut in a cage all day). Rover seeks Happiness by rubbing your leg until you've found the tin-opener, and then going to sleep. Adored Father strives for Happiness by dreaming of Writing His Novel but akshully spending all his time walling himself in, banging nails through his toes Etck, believing that in the midst of this Chaos, Swearing, Collapsing of DIY

Projects at approach of the first feather-duster Etck, lies an Inner Peace in which a man is Absolved By Honest Toil.

It's V. Dangerous to criticize other people's ways of Seeking Happiness, unless their idea of a Good Time happens to be World Domination, Raping, Pillaging Etck, which of course for many of the Most Famous and SUCCESSful Names in History it is. (This of course is a problem for Teenage Worriers, viz: so many of the Great Figures we learn about have such a weird idea of Happiness.)

However, dear Readers, have you spotted the Fly in the Ointment, the open manhole cover in the Journey of Life, the Iceberg threatening the blissful course of Leo and Katie?

You gottit. If everybody's Idea of Happiness is so different, how can every Yuman Being SUCCESSfully find much as possible of their own version without stepping on other people's? It wld make *moi* V. Happy to swear Undying Lurve and Devotion to Adam Stone but in my more sensible moments I have to consider a V. V. Tiny element of doubt that He might not feel the same. It might make *moi* Happy to grow a vast Tropical Rain Forest at the bottom of the garden full of exotic Boids, chattering monkeys, gerbils the size of badgers and strange undiscovered tribes who play wild, Urge-Awakening music that reunites you with yr Primal Being, but it wld not make Adored Parents happy when they get the letter from the Council, and the burning stake on the door from the neighbours.

Happiness is therefore a balance, between yr own needs and those of others. This is not to say that your Search for Happiness will not sometimes cause pain to Another (such as when you have to tell Eric Grovel in 9L that despite his Smile of Hope and geyser of perspiration when he sees you, and Valentine cards every day of the year, you think the two of you shld be Just Frendz) or that you may not occasionally need to be tough to be fair on both them and you. It's just that if you make a Habit of it, you may have an underlying desire to cause Unhappiness that can sometimes be caused by not liking Yrself as much as you think you do – and if that's the case you, or you and somebody who understands, shld maybe ask why.

HEALTH

It is V. Hard to be happy, or even slightly serene, or SUCCESSful in any way, if you feel ill all the time, so eating well, exercising a bit, sleeping enough and not poisoning yr bod with evile crazed drugges is V. V. Imp.

If you feel that you are excessively Worried about yr health and go to doc's thinking you have brain tumour Etck every other week or find yrself looking up 'sore throat' in book of symptoms and convincing yrself it's meningitis, you could, just possibly, be a hypochondriac. I shld know (blush, guilt at bothering NHS who shld be caring for terminally ill pensioners. And did they *really* check that pimple out? Could it be a . . . tumour!? Etck). Try V. Hard to make yourself forget about these Worries for a year. You can do it (I've managed not to consult dictionary of symptoms for eight whole daze so far and am feeling much more Worried, I mean, much better for it).

Hobbies

Moi, I find that a SUCCESSful cure for Worry is when I'm involved in hobbies. When I was nine, it was collecting model horses and making little saddles and bridles for them. When I was ten, I briefly involved myself in forgery (fivers, stamps, ol letters that I tried to sell to newspapers pretending they were from Stalin Etck). And my lurve of football was legendary and V. Sadly nipped in bud by absence of opportunity and constant heartless jibes about my resemblance to goal-post Etck (whail, gnash, renting of nets Etck). But small SUCCESS in hobbies can be V. Rewarding, whether it's finally completing that 50,000 matchstick model of the *Titanic* or hand-rearing stag beetles. Go for it.

Hope

Essential ingredient for SUCCESS. Must cling on to shred of same, even when in deepest glume at failed SUCCESS, for there is always a new day Etck. Each time you get up, there is new HOPE; each time you open envelope, answer phone, open door Etck there is new HOPE. Each time you go out of house, you HOPE you might turn corner to see person-of-yr-dreams Etck. Do not approach postman in this frame of mind however as he is prob married with seventeen children. My frend Aggy's mother ran off with postman causing tragick family breakdown Etck.

Ideas

IDEAS from the Teenage Think Tank.
Teenage Wommns have best inventions
(but least dosh).

IGNORANCE

Huge and deadly force that deprives werld of life-enhancing spirit. True enemy of SUCCESS of all kinds. This is not just to do with bukes Etck but to do with understanding different people and cultures. It is the lack of understanding, and lack of listening, which as all Teenage Worriers know, is a V. Common fault with most Middle-aged Worriers, that leads to ignorance. The SUCCESSful blotting out of same can only be achieved by the exercise of . . .

IMAGINATION

Without which, no true SUCCESS is possible. You must be imaginative to understand problems and therefore solve them. You need imagination to write, to paint, to make anything at all. And it's making things that makes us who we are.

IMPERIALISM POWER DOMINATION and other V. Bad stuf

This is what Big SUCCESSful Nations do to little Nations. They conquer them first, and then try to squash all the thingz their people do that are different, so they might one day feel that giving all their best stuff to the big nation is just like keeping it in the family. But it never completely changes the minds of the conquered people, as the Romans found with us, and we found in doing it to lots of other people. The decline of the British Umpire has been sharp in recent years and it's amazing how well all the little Nations hung on to their traditions against the odds. This is not the kind of SUCCESS, I hardly need to say, admired by L. Chubb.

But Imperialists are cleverer now. Instead of taking over with Guns, whips, general Bossiness Etck, it is now done with Money. The USA for instance has V. Big Influence around the world not just because it has the most powerful army (though it does) but because people want Levi 501s, Mad Mikie Jackson records Etck, all the way from Bolivia to Bangalore. Investment or no investment by multi-nationals can now make or break little countries, as unconventional but V. Poor places like Nicaragua have found. A SUCCESSful world, such as most idealistic Teenage Worriers wld like to inhabit, will attempt to reverse these injustices, led by the Duchess of Chubb, naturally (I may find it in my heart to accept a title if House of Lords not abolished by the time they offer me one. Although I shall naturally do so with um, modest reluctance).

Intelligence

My big brother Ashley has loads of this and me and Benjy seem tragickly to have the mouse's share. My Only Mother wrings hands and wails, as she thinks it is cos Granny Gosling forked out to send Ashley to a posh school and she has therefore let her only daughter down. I agree that class sizes of about six little chaps with V. Pushy parents, tuba and yoga lessons Etck probably gave Ashley an advantage over *moi* but this is *education*, not *intelligence*. (I do have sneaky suspicion, however, that number of brain cells doled out by genetic inheritance Etck was V. Unfair, so that when Ashley got purrfect face, body, soul Etck, he also got more generous share of grey matter. If he weren't so V. Kind and understanding I wd hate him.)

Try to develop as much of the IQ-type intelligence that passes exams as you can. Choose the subjects best suited to your type of intelligence. Never mind that the exams are V. V. V. Narrow measurements, cos you need to pass some of them in order to get into a position of power from which to change them. BUT don't kid yourself that passing them makes you a Better Person or that people who don't are somehow worse than you. If you do, you'll forget all about changing them and start to think that the system works . . .

And try to develop as many other kinds of the other intelligences as you can – creativity, intuition, Enquiring Mind Etck. This will develop you as a whole and decent person who is capable of thinking fast and empathizing with those who don't.

JOBS

Fewer people in the UK are being more industrious than ever before, I reckon – in other words, running as fast as they can to take care of jobs that used to be done by three people and are now done by one V. Baggy-Eyed person and a desktop computer they could have run the moon programme from a few years ago. These changes mean that industry in the other sense – factories and stuff – is now in a V.

Sorry State in Little Britain, which is why so many people are V. Depressed and why Teenage Worriers are more Worried than their parents used to be at the same age, cos there are likelier to be fewer jobs in the future, unless Govt follows advice of Teenage Think Tank to share out werk properly.

Instead of You LOT working SIX DAYS and YOU OTHER LOT having NO work... You are ALL going to work THREE days

Hey!

yeah!

Why not?

N.B. Adults will tell you this V. simple idea won't work. But **WHY NOT?**

Multi-national companies now look at the world map and don't see people like you and me and our Adored or Appalling Parents but markets, and wage-costs; so they move businesses where they can get the job done most cheaply. Teenage Worriers now have to contemplate New Questions of Our Time like does it mean anything to be British (or French, or Dutch, or Eskimo), and how can I figure out which life Skill or Skills will be worth anything in the year 2010? If you have any answers to these Brain-Hurting issues, please contact the El Chubb Think Tank.

See also CAREERS. Which leads us naturally to . . .

JUGGLING

I do not mean clubs or balls, but juggling loads of different things at once (feeding Rover, getting to skule, placating worries of Only Mother, Benjy Etck, surveying spotz – my life is a nightmare of conflicting demands). Learning how to do this well is obviously wot differentiates the truly SUCCESSful Teenage Worriers from the slobs like *moi*. Must make list . . . argh, hopeless case, Worry. Etck.

KNOWLEDGE

Getting as much of this about as many things as possible is essential for SUCCESS. But getting a lot of it about one thing in particular is the key to mega-SUCCESS. Once you decide what you really want to do, you can not bother to learn about things you don't like. Sadly, when you are a Teenage Worrier you need to dip into everything as it's only by doing that that you can find out what you DON'T want as well as what you do. (At least I know for sure that I'm not going to be a pilot or a ballet dancer, so that's two things I can cross off vast list.)

I'll just give little eg of knowledge: let's take, say, (she says, pretending to pick something at random, but akshully going for own little obsession), *Horses*. If you want to show SUCCESSful knowledge about horses, harken to this: they are measured, not in cm, km or even feet and inches, but hands. Weird, huh? Their saddles, bridles, and other taming paraphernalia are all called Tack (which is short for tackle). When you brush them, it's called grooming and their hairbrushes are called things like Dandy brush and curry comb. So . . . if you hear some hearty type saying: 'Jolly fine filly, about 15 hands. Just off to get the dandy, the curry and the tack', you'll know what they're on about and won't think they've discovered some great new take-away caff.

I make this point cos this is one of the few things I know about. But it is easy to find out about anything you're truly interested in so, for 'horses', just substitute 'planetary systems', 'violin music' Etck and go and FIND OUT. Learning about ANYTHING AT ALL is key to SUCCESS.

LAUGHTER

If you can cast cares to winds, make light of heavy sorrows, laugh through yr tears, put on happy face, whistle happy tune, smile though yr heart is breaking Etck, you will stand better chance of SUCCESS in Life's journey Etck.

'Laugh and the World Laughs with you' may be a V. Good Saying but sometimes, a chuckle will do.

LIQUORICE

You may think you can skip this entry, but SUCCESSful life lessons come in surprising places, so read on. (Write in and complain if I am wrong.) Liquorice is a ghastly sweet, the extinction of which would not diminish the quality of life. If only the energy that goes into the making of liquorice went into the making of FUDGE then the werld would be a happier place. But wait, what is that distant cry? It is the cry of the *Glycyrrhiza glabra* farmers, whose leguminous plant forms the root from which liquorice is made. The gooey stuff also goes into medicines. Which goes to show that whatever you think, there is usually another point of view.

The apple the cloud the Kangaroo
Each has a different point of view

LOTTERY

Of course winning the Lottery wld make *moi* happier, but then I am a Teenage Worrier and we know what imaginative World-enhancing things we wld do with all that lovely dosh. The adults who win seem to just get more of the things that made them depressed in the first place – bigger houses to keep tidy, more sofas to worry about the colour of, vast gardens to fret about the weeding of, more slaves to moan about the unworthiness of . . . yachts they don't know how to sail or fix, holidays where they get sick of the food and sea-sick and home-sick. Then there's all the law-suits from ex-wives and children they never knew they had, old frendz they haven't seen for twenty years asking for a little something to tide them over, begging letters Etck, Etck.

MANNERS

Being polite is obv helpful in being SUCCESSful. Nobody likes rude young bats who shoulder them aside at bus stops Etck and although the world of Middle-aged Worriers is full of such people who got big by being bossy, El Chubb believes (or at least hopes) that Teenage Worriers will build a world

where people can be both SUCCESSful AND caring.
'Manners don't cost anything' says Granny Chubb.
If only today's yoof could educate their parents
about this, how much better and more dignified a
world it wld be . . . sigh. Even so, I bet Hitler knew
how to use a knife and fork, so manners are not a V.
Good guide to the SOUL.

MARTIAL ARTS

El Chubb has often wondered, it has to be said, what
all this eastern Bruce Lee stuff, like ballet with
muggings, has to do with being a Better Person,
becoming more sympathetic to old ladies, working
out why yr family are all Psychos Etck. However,
that's the very Prob. In the west, we spend all the
time we aren't out causing havoc, intervening all
over the place, making Big Decisions Etck, trying to
work out in our Hedz how we can do Better
Intervening, make Bigger Decisions and so forth.
But in the eastern philosophies of Taoism and Zen
Buddhism, they reckon you should spend all the
time you currently spend thinking, practising how
to be better at *un*thinking instead. Then yr Body
and yr Mind Become One, so that in combat you
instantly respond without thought, and all other
times like going to the Loo, cleaning the gerbil-cage
Etck, you are in a spiritual state of balance in which
there isn't a You inside and a World outside. I have

to say that if the contents of above gerbil's cage are akshully part of *moi* rather than disagreeable elements of an External Werld then I may end up a bigger Teenage Worrier than I am now, but perhaps it's unwise to go into the details of these things.

BUT if I cld achieve this balance it wld obv be V. SUCCESSful in terms of self-defence, a vital need for today's Urban Teenage Worriers.

Money

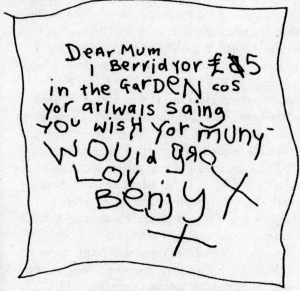

Dear Mum
I Berrid yor £5
in the GaRDEN cos
yor arlwais saing
YOU wisH yor muny
WOUld gro
LOV
BenjY X
X

Just one of my beloved family's
many financial disasters.
The fiver was never found.

If you have opened a bank account you will now know that Staff in banks spend a lot of time wishing you a nice weekend, apologizing for the delay, sweeping red carpet before Yr every step Etck, but if you owe them the equivalent of a drop in the ocean of their hoarded zillions that they weren't expecting you to owe them they change V. Quickly and tell you to cough up or they'll get the ladz round to nick yr video. Banks, though, are now V. Imp to students because the Govt has encouraged them to finance student loans which means that for half of yr life you are working for them instead of for Yr Dreamz, nearest and dearest Etck. This is all part of a conspiracy called the World Banking System, in which the same principle is applied to developing countries very like El Chubb. The World Banks basically give student loans to poor, undeveloped, snuffly-nosed, skinny countries like *moi* to encourage them to learn how to be big, glossy, shiny-nosed, respectable countries like my posh frend Hazel's dad. The little countries aren't sure how to do it, or sure if they want to, so the Banks demand about twenty times their money back to help them concentrate, and encourage multi-nationals to build factories there so that they can get lots of cars, computers Etck built for tuppence. To get everyone a fair bite of werld's cherry, we have to stop all this rubbidge and not ask for our money back. SUCCESS means giving up as well as getting.

The search for money of your own, though, is

something of an obsession for Teenage Worriers, espesh if like Hazel, you are surrounded by rich kids who all get allowances from their V. Rich Paters and Maters (this is Latin for parents, as Ashley has often pointed out to poor ignorant, comprehensively-educated *moi*). But I am determined to make own dosh and not rely on hand-outs, from parents or anyone (chance wld be a fine thing with my parents anyway, wail, moan, cries of 'It's not fair' Etck). Am trying to revive old hobby by forging old-looking fivers as we speak, with help of V. Good new computer programme that scans notes and prints them out. V. Hard to get watermark right . . .

NB If you want to both understand money and make it, Accountancy is a career worth considering as Accountants are for V. Rich people to help them avoid paying money to the Government to educate the likes of *moi*, Build A Just Society Etck, and save up money to educate the likes of themselves, Build A Vast Mansion with Three Swimming Pools Etck. Hence, if you become an accountant you will have big cheques from rich people as long as you can kid them you are helping to make them richer.

Please don't get IMPRESSION I am OBSESSED with MONEY. I just like to doodle (blush)

NEGATIVITY

If you have V. negative 'glass is half empty' as opposed to positive 'glass is half full' attitude to life it may be hard to entrap the elusive glimmerings of SUCCESS.

My own family is V. Dysfunctional in this respect as we are all whingeing victims of Fate, except Ashley. Hence: Only Mother moans about how she used to be swimming in dosh until she married my penniless father. Adored Father moans about how nobody understands the travails of a working class novelist who had to look after his penniless mother. Benjy moans about the floors, the dark, the light, school, food, his clothes Etck. And I am as you know V. Put upon having a father who won't werk, a mother who won't cook and a brother who won't shut up. Am making V. Big resolution to look on Bright side Etck and pursue goals in orderly fashion blaming no-one but myself if I go wrong. If I'd been brought up in sane family it wld be much easier, moan whinge, there I go again . . .

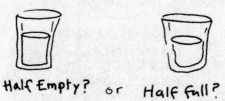

Half Empty? or Half Full?

NEW THINGS

Embrace the New! Also embrace the old! But do not be scared of things. I only wish I had been taught to try out new stuff instead of being lumbered with a neurotic mother who told me to be careful every time I went outside the front door . . . New experiences, as long as they are legal, are almost always rewarding Etck. Even if you don't fancy scuba diving, if you get the chance, go! (But do not embrace the shark, er and remember to wear a wet suit and . . . Worry, worry)

OYSTERS

V. Expensive 'delicacy' eaten by SUCCESSful people with more money than sense (as Granny Chubb wld say). I wld never eat an oyster after reading *The Walrus and the Carpenter* because I cld never forget Lewis Carroll's haunting lines:

> *'What think you, little oysters?'*
> *But answer came there none.*
> *And this was scarcely odd because*
> *they'd eaten every one.*

The betrayal of Trust in this great pome seared
my eleven-year-old heart when first I read it and has
left its mark for eternity. I draw the line at white-
bait, too. Too many little lives in one mouthful.

PHONES

Brrrrrrrrrrrrr Brrrr

Mobile phones are always carried by people who
want to look SUCCESSful. V. V. SUCCESSful
people do not need them however as instead they
have a faithful army of minions who answer all their
calls for them. I hope to be one of these before too
long (not the minion, the SUCCESSful person). But
does this big improvement in ability to
commoonicate make us Happier and more
SUCCESSful people? Discuss.

Sound makes me with anticipation. *No wonder this makes me SHIVER*

TIP
If desperate or broke (or both!), you can always
borrow small sibling's toy mobile phone which has
V. Convincing ring.

POETRY

It is V. Touching that so many Teenage Worriers
write poems and it is V. Good for the soul to do so,
but – I hate to say this – not many of the poems are
actually V. Good. You only have to read some of

those middle-aged Worriers poems that are printed up in real-look leatherette by cheapskate publishers and then sold to the authors for £35 to see that this is not a talent that necessarily improves with age. If you want to impress and are not too sure of your own skill, why not use a poem from one of the Truly Grates? You can go for ye Big Old names: Shakespeare (lots of love sonnets, many of them to a boy if you want poem for yr BeLurved), Marlowe Etck, or try more modern stuff like Roger McGough, Benjamin Zephaniah, Murray Lachlan Young Etck. There are loads of collections.

Aaah POETRY, Roses, ROMANCE tra-la LA

Politics

Really SUCCESSful Politicians are Good Listeners, sez El Chubb. I reckon they're the ones who can hear what people different to them are talking about (Teenage Worriers, frinstance, but also poor people, those speaking different languages Etck Etck) and balance it against all the other Stuff going on in Society, so the Laws Etck reflect the needs of as many people as Poss. So if you want true SUCCESS in politics, rather than just crude old power, this is what you shld be like.

Just a few questions

* <u>Samples:</u>

1   When did you last queue for a bus?

2   When did you last pick your kids up from school?

3   When did you last wash a sock?

4   When did you last wash a pair of socks?

5   Do you think financial advisers should earn more than nurses?

   (Etck. Etck. make up your own)

POSITIVE THINKING

LIFE-TIP: If you feel you have a tendency to look on down-side, remember El Chubb's two fave sayings: *Life is just a bowl of Cherry stones* and *When one door closes, another door closes.*

If you can do better than this, award yrself small life-enhancing treat ie: a single Smartie.

> My dad killed my Mum. I've had 19 foster families. I'm due in court on Monday. I've never had a Best Friend or a pet and I've never seen the sea. BUT, the sun is shining, I have a pen, paper, shampoo, food. I am definitely better off than V. Big number of people in the world and I am going to IMPROVE EVERYBODY'S LIVES

Er, this Teenage Worrier is V. Good example of Positive Thinking (guilt, writhe, mone...)

PULLING STRINGS

Er my cousin's friend's aunt's daughter worked for you five years ago and suggested I give you a ring

SUCCESSful Middle-aged Worriers often call this networking, which is a polite way of saying they go to parties Etck in order to toady up to more SUCCESSful people than themselves in case they need them later. Obviously, if you have rich SUCCESSful parents who can put a word in the right ear of bank manager, werld leader, newspaper editor Etck you are in with a much better chance than the majority of Teenage Worriers who have to bumble along making it up as they go. I think this is V. Unfair, but then life often is V. Unfair and will continue to be until werld is run by *moi* (power-mad visions of domination Etck).

So, if you have frendz or contacts of any kind in the kind of jobz you are looking for, it does make sense to get in touch. People like to work with people they know, and will be V. Likely at least to give you a small opportunity to show what you can do. So don't be shy of pulling strings if you are lucky enough to have any to pull (sigh, chance wld be a fine thing Etck).

QUESTIONING

SUCCESS depends on asking the right questions at the right time, viz: if I drop this heavy weight on my foot, will it ruin my chances of being footballer? Without the ability to ask and answer questions, you will not get far down yr chosen path. Questioning also means not just accepting the answer you're given, viz:

Can I have a job?
No.
Why?
Because you're not suitable.
Why not?
Because you're too stupid, young, inexperienced, lazy (Etck).
Why do you say that?
Because it's true.
It's not, let me show you.

NB Confidence is necessary for above. Practise in front of mirror and don't take no for an answer.

Racism

If you feel yr SUCCESS in finding work or frends is due to your colour, you shld immediately report it to Race Relations authorities. There is obv no hope of a SUCCESSful country that goes on discriminating against people for these krap reasons, but it does still happen. If you suspect it, always ask why? The person who you think is being racist will be V. Embarrassed if it's true.

NO HUMANS

NO BLUE EYED PEOPLE IN HERE

KEEP OUT IF YOU'RE TALL

WE HATE anyone with small TEETH

unless they believe what some other V. stupid person has told them. Why not see if they agree with the signs above

Rewards

You need rewards for SUCCESS. If yr skule doesn't believe in them, try to persuade the teachers that they are encouraging things to get and be sure to pat yrself on back when you know you have done something as well as you can. It is V. V. Good for Soul to do so and anything that boosts self-confidence is good for SUCCESS in general.

School

SUCCESS at skule can be broken down into the following areas:

1) with frendz

Does anyone in the whole Skule **LIKE** me?

2) in sport

3) in some work

$2 + 2 = 22$ ✗
$3 + 3 = 33$ ✗

4) with teachers

WHO said that?

5) in exams

Arghhhhh!

If you do not feel that you are a winner in any of these areas, pick the one you are most likely to succeed with and concentrate on it till it gets a teeny bit better. Then go on to another. Then go back to the first. Then try a third. Then go back to the second. Don't try for all five cos V. Few Teenage Worriers can manage all of them. But aim, by the time you leave, to feel good about *one* of these areas and possibly two.

Sexism

As in racism above, sexism is still a force to be reckoned with as boyz look at yr chest rather than yr soul Etck (not the case with *moi*, who has no chest . . .) and when you get out into werld, you can still, if a gurl, hit yr head on glass ceiling when you discover all the best jobz and dosh are still going to blokes. This is improving, but quite slowly, despite wot the newspapers say about babes taking power.

Spirituality

Adored Father told me once about a play in which a physicist keeps a lucky horseshoe on the door of his laboratory, and then when all his clever mates laugh at him he says he doesn't believe in it really. 'But,' he says, 'they say it goes on working even if you don't believe it.' I don't wish to imply that I think religion is the same as superstition, but it seems to *moi* that the need for the Yuman Race to have religions is V. Closely related to it. The V. Famous psychoanalyst Sigmund Freud (Espesh Famous for thinking SEX was behind everything, and in front of it too, though less so in the case of some of us than others, moan, whinge, examine tape-measure suspiciously Etck) thought Religion was just a symptom of how much we repress all our Dark Thoughts, and when the Yuman Race grew up and learned to live with what goes on in the Inner Recesses of Ye Minde, we'd all just grow out of it.

Also Karl Marx, the Famous German Thinker of V. Clever Thoughts and founder of Marx & Spenders (I made that bit up — L. Chubb) said Religion was the Opium of the People, and was just there to make the Poor and Needy keep their mouths shut and not grumble, because God had decided they should live like that and it was Just Tough — God is therefore V. Convenient for the rich people who hope the poor won't get so fed up about their circs that they try to take their dosh off them Etck.

For *moi*self, I am inclined to think that while a lot of V. Horrible things have certainly been done in the name of various kinds of gods, a lot of V. Horrible things have also been done in the name of Yuman Beings people treated as if they were gods, viz: Hitler Etck. Maybe this means we do have a need to give ourselves up to something beyond the world inside our own Hedz, and which makes us Feel United With Others, and praps it's better if we accept that and try to do something positive with it, rather than forgetting about it until the next shouting loony shows up with a uniform and a gun. I believe that most SUCCESSful people have some kind of spiritual life, as it is V. Nourishing and can take them away from rigours of workplace Etck.

SPORT

SUCCESS in ye fields of sport is sought after by nearly all male and lots of female Teenage Worriers, but after you get out of skule it becomes a lot less important, so if you are one of those completely weedy people who can't see ball to hit it Etck, take heart, your failings will not be noticed for the rest of yr life. Nonetheless, sport is V. Good for you, V. Good for character-building stuff like learning to lose gracefully Etck as well as learning to compete (essential part, sadly, of striving for SUCCESS).

CAMPAIGN for more sports fields in tragickly underfunded skules. CAMPAIGN for gurlz football! Get fit and don't be wimpy (wish I could) . . .

Tragick... V. Big waste of my only TALENT. Just think if only my Junior SKULE had gone and given gurlz more of a chance... gwme moan, whinge.....

Example of Moi being V. good sport about wasted football talent Etck. (If I had played, Werld Kup wld be ours... Etck Etck).

Stardom

By now, you shld have an idea that El Chubb is not interested in being a STAR. I wld hate to be followed by seedy journalists with vast lenses watching me pick my hooter and seeing contents of same Etck. So if stardom is what you want, you may have wrong buke. Trying to be good at something may occasionally lead to stardom (ie: Acting) but if you get it, you are almost bound to regret it. Aim to earn loads of dosh but keep low profile is El Chubb's advice. Write to yr favourite star and ask if they enjoy it. That shld put you off, except they are bound to lie . . .

Tidiness

Return of the lost SOCK

Some Middle-aged Worriers seem to think that organization is key to SUCCESS, and I have sneaky feeling that, apart from painters, poets Etck who can live in hovels happy only with their ART, they may be right.

I blame my own tragick disorganization on the fact that my only parents are so V. Lazy and sluttish. My Adored Father is surrounded by festering piles of old newspapers that he insists on keeping for his DIY articles and my mother barely washes a cup by

How to TIDY UP

(part 402)

Get THREE boxes or binbags
Label 1, 2, 3.

1. Chuck **OUT**
2. Give to JUMBLE
3. Keep to **SORT** later

GUIDE TO CATEGORIES

1. Bits of fluff, dried up
   pens, odd socks, old gum,
   bus tickets, small bits
   of plastic. Anything
   broken.

2. Anything NOT broken
   you no longer need
   or want.

3. Everything else.

Now - all you should have
left is yr bed, cupboard
Etck. There shld be
NOTHING on the
floor (If only it were
so easy. Sigh).

Moi: failing to follow own advice.

waving it under the tap and shaking it, or sometimes running an oil-painty finger over it for especially deep down stains. However, I look at Ashley, whose room, though tiny, gleams like new pin, and realize that it is just that I am a Bad person . . . moan, glume (*Get on with it – Ed*).

Question: Is tidiness genetic? Did Granny Chubb's genes skip my dad and go straight into Ashley, bypassing *moi*? Wld my mother be more tidy Etck if she hadn't had nannies and cleaners running after her picking up each sock and crumb when she was a mere child? Whatever the answer, the tragick consequences of our family history (or herstory as I'm sure all gurlz shld call their lives) is that my Only Mother, having been bought up in conditions like Royal Family Etck, cannot get used to living in slum. Thus, though incapable of doing hand's turn herself, she is always nagging the rest o us. I am now quite an expert at burning fish finger and turning sprouts to green liquid just like her . . We certainly miss Ashley, who used to cook family supper every night, using a proper cookbook (and couple of saucepans, arf arf) but now he has swanne off to University to save werld, we can only wait ar hope that Benjy may have a cooking gene. He trie to cook his hamster once, so there may be a glimm of hope . . .

Umbrella

Someone once said that a bank is something that will give you an umbrella in fine weather and ask for it back when it rains. SUCCESS is a bit like that. When you are doing well, you tend to do better and better, cos you believe in yrself and so people believe in YOU, and fall over themselves to help you Etck. When you do badly, the whole thing goes into reverse. So, think of that umbrella and always try to have something to fall back on in yr self-esteem buke if one part of your SUCCESS-strategy fails . . . Arg.

Vocals

Yr voice just could be the key to yr SUCCESS, since we live in V. Unfair werld, where high-pitched whine of mosquito is less enchanting to ear than deep buzz of honey bee Etck. Sadly it's sometimes not what you say, but the way that you say it, as Decrepit mangey old class (or clarse) system in Little Britain still rules and oppresses the majority oo carn't speak proper. What El Chubbo has noticed, however, is how the way the Upper clarse people speak has changed over the years. If you look at V. Old Brit movies (as I have been doing in an attempt

to prepare for my magnificent film career) or even early TV ads, you will notice that even V. Ordinary folk like suburban housewives dusting already immaculate banisters speak with a plum the size of Buckingham Palace in their mouths and a chandelier where their tonsils ought to be. eg: *hice* for 'house', *gawn* for 'gone' Etck. Only the Royal Family speak like that today . . . but it is significant that society is still in thrall to crippling snobbery re lingo. And as it still seems that speaking posh can impress people in Powerful positions, it cld be an idea to brush up your accent until you are powerful and then CAMPAIGN V. V. Haaaard for end to this Snobbery, viz: Only V. Nice, Welsh, Caribbean, and Cockney accents can get power for next five hundred years.

WEDDINGS

Some Teenage Worriers think it a sign of SUCCESS to get married. (Obviously, it is more of a sign of SUCCESS to ackshully *stay* married.) To *moi*, it seems an odd dream to long to wear daft clothes, to make a bunch of impossible promises in full view of a throng of distant relatives you've never met, snog in front of said grisly throng, sign yr life away, get pissed and go off on holiday being pelted with paper, horseshoes, fake foam Etck. From this you're supposed to Live happily Ever After?

Weddings usually start with engagements, which used to be arranged by parents largely for reasons of property, links with other families Etck, which led to great abuses. Eventually the church made it illegal to arrange the betrothal of children under seven (!) but Arranged Marriages are still quite common in many cultures and as yet I don't know if anyone's done a survey of which kind of marriages are happier . . .

NB El Chubb's tip for a SUCCESSful marriage: you shld just live together for the first twenty years or so and then make an honest man or woman of each other (still wish only parents had tied the knot though, so not sure if this is right. Aargh.)

WISHING-ON-A-STAR

Wells, stars, wishbones, birthday cakes, little blokes calling themselves Rumplestilstkin, strange old bats posing as fairy godmothers — all these play their part in the process called growing up. Pretty soon you realize none of it works, but you go on anyway. And why not? Keeping hope alive is one of the vital keys to SUCCESS in everything you do, dear fellow struggler in the vineyards of Worry, so keep wishing, cos without wishes and hopes you're nowhere.

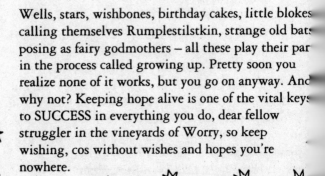

Xcellence

OK. I'll admit Xcellence has its part to play in the game of SUCCESS but the famous phrase goes: * 'Lucky? Yeah. The harder I work, the luckier I get.' And that's the point: Xcellence on its own isn't enough — there's got to be V. Hard work too. There's no point, frinstance, in having a talent for drawing unless you draw all the time and improve it. Excellence is usually 10% talent and 90% devotion. Even those incredibly few people of real genius are almost always obsessed by what they do and do it all the time. El Chubb, being a nachurally V. Lazy soul, preaches equal amounts of hanging out, gazing at navel type daydreaming time in order to pursue crazed luny obsessions . . . For it must be remembered that even the geniuses are often not discovered till they are pushing up daisies, so knowing how to be Happy is more important for a SUCCESSful life than knowing how to be clever. Think of poor old Van Gogh, wandering about with only one ear and never selling a painting. And now his sunflowers, and even copies of his sunflowers, sell for small fortune (sob).

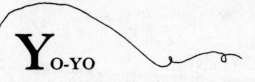

Yo-yo

Learn to let go. SUCCESS and failure follow each other as surely as Spring follows Winter. One thing is working, another thing isn't. One door closes, another door closes, blah blah. Most SUCCESSful people truly believe that another door opens, they really do. And for them, it seems to happen. So when you're picked for the skule footie team only to break your leg on the day of the match, or when the results of the Art Competition everyone said you'd win come through and you are not even mentioned in the list of 300 highly recommended entries, DO NOT EVER despair. SUCCESS is not something to take personally. It wafts its wings skittishly, only to swoop elsewhere. Your life is about trying to get it in four main areas: werk, home, people, self. The greatest of these (cos it helps all the others to happen) is self. Not selfishness, but self-esteem. This, sadly, is an item that El Chubb, and most Teenage Worriers, are V. V. Low in. And one knock can send us flying off perch. El Chubb's advice is to read about lives of others. See how V. Complicated, V. Full of highs and lows most lives are and decide that you won't be knocked down by adversity but will struggle up and fight on, so that the yo-yo of life will be buzzing up the string and never dangling at the bottom for too long. To achieve this wondrous state you need . . .

ZEST

Zest is that stuff on outside of orange and lemon peel. Bitter, but zingy. Zest for life is almost universal in SUCCESSful folk: they are doers, triers, smilers, singers, dreamers, thinkers. Having a zest for anything means you are never bored, so even if you live in slum, have no dosh, are abandoned by everyone you care for, if there's one thing you love doing, it can keep your zest for life aflame . . . Find it, nourish it, dearest Teenage Worriers, and the future will be golden path up which you will cheerfully stumble.

FORWARD TO WILD SUCCESS!

AFTERWORD

And now, dearest fellow Teenage Worriers, I reach the end of this humble survey of SUCCESS. I look at my own small life in the vast cosmos of the Yuniverse and I say to myself: Does any of it matter? Does it really matter if I get a single GCSE? Does it matter whether Benjy ever stops worrying about floors? Does it matter if my Adored Father leaves home with another acrobat or my Only Mother hits bottle in despair at fact that she has spent twenty years trying to paint and can still barely hold brush? Does it matter that my own head is a mass of matted phobias, crossed wires and festering worry about V. Small things and V. Large things with no clear line between them? The answer to these questions is, like yr own Life, both . . .

> *Yes*
> *and*
> *No.*

The Yes bit is about SUCCESS. It's about trying to unfurl the bit you can unfurl and using all the positive bits you've got to make everything as good as you possibly can.

The No bit is also about SUCCESS. It's about not caring too much about the things you can't change (so that you can concentrate on the things you can).

And so, my dear reader, turn the page and why not fill in this little summary of yr SUCCESSes now. Put it away for ten years and look at it again then, or even fill it in again? You could do it every ten years, until you are sixty, or seventy, or eighty, or ninety, and see whether a little bit of what you hoped to achieve has happened. And if you get to ninety, you will be SUCCESSful at at least one thing: Living a long life! But what I think will happen is that things that bug you now will have changed in ten or twenty years time, so you can hardly remember WHY they were so important, but that hobbies you cherish now will continue to give you happiness for ever . . .

I end with the following wish: may all yr happy dreams come true and all yr nightmares crumble into dust. And may the rainbow-coloured birdy of SUCCESS lay its egg on your doorstep! (Must put pillow in front of door in case . . .)

Lurve,

×

× *Letty Chubb*

Date – and YEAR

Name: Age:

What I wish for MOST in MY life NOW

What I wish for MOST in MY future

What I wish for MOST in the WORLD

What I would MOST like to DO

Things I am PROUD of

Things I hope to AVOID

What I enjoy doing most NOW

The people and hobbies I care about MOST Now

What makes me sad

What makes me glad